Table of Contents

"Let's Ask Dad"

Wit, Wisdom, and Positive Encouragement

By: Billy F. Hopkins Jr.

About the Author

I'm a pretty simple man with some pretty simple thoughts on life. Being a realist can sometimes be a problem though. It causes me to question those who have lost touch with reality about day-to-day life and expectations of children in the athletic arena. I love all of my children and think they are the best at everything they do. However, I keep those thoughts to my children and myself. Why? Because I'm a realist! I know the chances of my kids being the most successful, most talented, superhero-like athlete, student, employee, or even person are slim at best. I'll never tell them that! All they need to know is that I love them and whatever their accomplishments, in my eyes, they are the best ever.

I've done my time in retail, entrepreneurship, sales, wholesale, and the school of hard knocks. I now live out my passion by playing what I call, "Are You Smarter Than A 5th Grader?" every day. I bring a unique view of learning from life experiences in business to a common sense approach of application in a classroom.

I never expect perfection from anyone, but I do expect perfect effort. I will never ask someone to give 110% when 100% is all they will ever have at their disposal. Just give that! One last thought, "Practice does NOT make perfect!" My belief is this, "Perfect practice makes perfect. Otherwise, practice only makes permanent!"

I desire to do three things in life. Love God! Love People! Serve others!

Motivation to Lean Forward

I often wonder when you get closer to the finish line, do you begin to lose the motivation that once drove you to continue in the race? As I get closer to finishing my goals I wonder if I have experienced some form of "burnout," or if the light burning bright at the end of the tunnel is actually an oncoming train. Maybe when you complete one chapter in life you're required to turn the page to begin another, tuck a bookmark inside to hold your place, or slowly close the book and willingly give up on your goals and dreams.

We are told throughout life to stand our ground and never back down. But when we drive a stake in the ground or draw a line in the sand, aren't we subconsciously saying, "I'm tethered right here where

I stand protecting this one area of my life?" Or better yet, are we content in defending one side of this so called boundary we've etched in the earth that we spend our lives daring others to cross and face the consequences?

Being comfortable or unmoving in life can often be the biggest hindrance to making a change or striving for something better. I know, as a football fan, if the runner decides to quit moving his legs and stands straight up where he has stopped, he hasn't merely said, "This is where I choose to stop, and I am satisfied with what gains I have made." In reality, his actions will cause him to be driven backwards and most likely punished for his complacency. Being comfortable where I am cannot be an option. We should always strive to lean forward so that if we fall flat on our faces, we will have at least gained some ground.

Is it the end, or the beginning?

Life seems to move so quickly at times, yet at other times it seems to move so slowly! When you take on a task that seems almost overwhelming, you always look for the end of the journey. The end of the journey seems to be so distant when, in reality, it is just a moment away. For a life that lasts less than a vapor in time, the mountain that you are facing today is merely a small challenge that can be overcome with a simple footstep. In comparison to the big picture we call life, it is nothing more than an annoying speed bump in the road.

I have continually looked for the light at the end of the tunnel concerning my education. But in reality, that isn't the end. It is only the beginning! It is the closing of one chapter and the opening of another. When does the end come? Never! Life and death is a continuum. It will continue on for eternity. Without a gap, this thing we call life moves to eternity: eternal life or eternal death within a blink of an eye.

When you get frustrated with how long it is taking to get to the end of your journey, take a deep breath because it is moving much quicker than you ever imagined. When you wish your life away hoping to get to the end of your education, the end of your task at hand, the end of your journey, or the end of your career, remember, it is only the beginning. The beginning of the next sentence, the next paragraph, the next page, the next chapter, the next book, the next ever-writing journey of life! Live life as if each day is a new beginning! You'll enjoy the journey much more in the end!

Sticks, Stones, and Words All Hurt

On the playground you might hear the words, "Sticks and stones may break my bones, but words will never hurt me!" I think it should go a little like this, "Sticks and stones may cause temporary physical damage, but the effects of words can last a lifetime." I remember as a child that I would dance around those who called me names and repeat that mantra over and over again. I guess I was trying to convince myself that the saying was true.

Everyone reacts to things differently in life. Some people truly have developed the attitude that no matter what someone says to them, those words mean absolutely nothing. Others base their very existence from moment to moment on what others think and say about them. Those philosophies hold true for both children and adults alike. I have met many adults who are still dealing with harsh words spoken to them as small children and now, some 30 years later, the struggle is still real. Others could look someone in the eye, hear many negative words slung maliciously at them, and then turn and walk away as if they were made of Teflon.

My older children all had different ways of processing words spoken to them. In my attempt to train them up, I could swat one of their hands if they were doing something wrong or dangerous and they would sob as if their entire world had just ended. Yet another one would look at me like, "Really? Did you need something or are you just trying to keep me from having fun?" What I found for all of them was that a positive word placed strategically in their lives made all the difference in the world. However, words mean much more to some than others. Brianna was that child! Corporal punishment would've never been productive with her. As a matter of fact, she had all of her siblings convinced that spankings did not hurt her. She explained to them that she had mastered the art of receiving a spanking. In order to eliminate the pain, she explained, you simply tighten your butt cheeks. And in all seriousness, several of my children actually proclaimed that spankings were unfair because Brianna's spankings never hurt her. Brianna must've been pretty convincing!

Discipline is different for all of us as well. Brianna has always spoken the love language of words. Although she would often tell you she didn't care what others said about her, there was still noticeable hurt that would seep through if she had been wounded by a malicious word spoken. The same goes for her reaction to discipline. If she even thought I was disappointed in her, she would be deeply wounded. I learned very early in her upbringing, that disciplining this strong-willed child was going to take a different approach. Brianna was often hard headed and would push boundaries to their limits, but I knew that in order to help her mature and become a better adult, I would have to change my methods. I would have to become a wordsmith of positive and encouraging words if I were to carve out a place of influence that could possibly last into adulthood.

Into the later teen years and adulthood, Brianna would step out and attempt to spread her wings. Of course, that is exactly what you want for your children. You want them to be able to fly on their own. However, you also want them to be safe in their journey and not leave the nest prematurely. I would constantly remind her that if she stepped out from the protection of my umbrella, she would be vulnerable to heartbreak and emotional wounds. The only thing I could rely on was reminding her who she was created to be and what tremendous value she had in the eyes of God. In her relationships, I would constantly challenge her to have the mindset that she is the grand prize when it comes to dealing with young men. I explained to her that too many guys try to push toward a physical relationship rather than following the Lord's plan for relationships. The wonderful thing about Brianna was that she had become a woman who sought to keep her daddy happy, but more importantly she sought to please her heavenly Father and prepare herself for her future husband. My contentment came from seeing her bloom into a Godly young lady, while God loved seeing her chase after him.

The secret weapon? Words! The Bible talks about blessing and cursing being unable to come from the same well. Just like freshwater and saltwater have to come from two different sources, speaking words of blessing is always the better choice because these words heal and bring health and joy. Sticks and stones do hurt, but words hurt more. You need to be someone who knows and understands what words your Father in heaven has already spoken over you. Only then will you understand that those sticks, stones, and words are nothing compared to the words of life, words of joy, and words of healing that come from the one who is known as the Word, Jesus.

The Christmas Tree Breakdown

In the produce business, you have to take action when the opportunity presents itself. Produce, like tomatoes, bananas, grapes, and other fruits and vegetables has a very limited shelf life. I always refer to it as a "move-it-or-lose-it" business. If you don't move it off the shelf quickly, then you will be throwing it away and eating the loss both financially and physically. This is a business that can push you to making foolish decisions if you are not patient and wise. The stock market probably doesn't fluctuate as quickly as produce prices change on the wholesale market. Prices change with the mention of bad weather. Let them predict a freeze in California and prices will automatically adjust on the shelves across the country. A case of lettuce can cost ten dollars in the morning, rise to forty dollars by lunch, and still be part of the same batch of stock.

Christmas trees are commonly sold through produce markets and retailers. These sales have always been a huge part of our winter business for those few weeks between Thanksgiving and Christmas. It is a constant guessing game for those who play. Do the customers want large trees, fat trees, skinny trees, tall trees, short trees, or is this the year they decide to purchase an artificial tree? Trying to determine how many trees to have on hand from week to week is difficult at best. You need enough trees to offer a good selection, but you don't want so many trees that you are left with many still in stock when Christmas is over. Losing even a handful of fresh cut trees can cost you into the hundreds of dollars.

Christmas tree customers need quantity to select the perfect tree for their needs. They are some of the most fickle and persnickety customers you could ever face. They are looking for the "perfect" Christmas tree. The tree with absolutely no flaws, no bare spots, the perfect height, width, and color. This is Christmas, and everything has to be picture perfect.

One particular year, sales had gone a little better than projected, and the selection had become minimal at best. A trip to the supplier was a must in order to stay on top of the sales this year. It was the prime selling time, and we could not afford to stumble at this point in the game. This need would require a late night trip to the Farmer's Market, but that was acceptable because it never closed. The produce business is a twenty-four hour industry. This is a tangible version of the stock market. Buying low and selling high is a philosophy that knows no concept of time for the opportunist. This particular year the decision was made, the trip was a must, and someone had to make it happen now!

It was nearly 10:00 p.m. when I pulled away from the market in our large truck heading to the market with two helpers in tow. Brianna and Dawson wanted to make this late night run with me. This was not unusual because they had both grown up riding in the big truck with daddy, and each trip was sure to be fun and adventurous. This late night run would have its share of adventure, but the adventure we discovered on this trip was not fun at all.

We made the nearly 45 minute run toward the Farmer's Market which was located in a very rough area of town. One of those areas that, during the daylight hours, appeared to be a fairly safe place to be. However, when the sun went down, most people in this section of town went inside or to another part of town. As we pulled off the interstate, the truck began to make some unexpected noises, the engine light came on, an obnoxious rattle began, the truck shook, and smoke bellowed from under the hood. The truck rolled to a stop in the middle of the road right next to a truck stop that was known to be a magnet for prostitutes, drug dealers, and opportunists also know as thieves. We were now sitting ducks and could possibly be "easy-picking" for those lurking in the darkness of night.

I made a call to my dad who had always been our resident mechanic. It was nearly 11:00 p.m. now and finding parts to repair anything at this time of the night would be virtually impossible. I looked around again and realized our best option was for us to abandon the truck and get to a well-lit parking lot. There was a fast food restaurant on the opposite side of the street, and we quickly moved there. I was doing my best to keep the kids from seeing the fear that seemed to be grabbing me around the throat. We stepped up and ordered something to eat to pass the time as we waited for my dad to arrive. The kids settled in, and I saw a wrecker pull up to the truck. The first thought that ran through my mind was, "This is a wrecker sent by the city to tow the truck out of the road and directly to the city wrecker yard." I ran out to the road and was quickly greeted by the tow-truck driver with the following: "This is a dangerous situation you are in." I said, "I'm sorry, I tried to get the truck out of the main flow of traffic but it's just too heavy to push." The driver said, "The traffic is the least of your worries." He began hooking onto the truck, and I was thinking that dad probably didn't want the truck being hauled away. He worked frantically and sort of dismissed my presence until he said, "Hop in!" I told him that I couldn't leave because I had two children sitting in the restaurant across the street, and I was waiting for someone to come pick us up. He pointed to a building that was located right next to the crime-infested parking lot and said, "I'm going to put your truck right there because they have lights and cameras all over the building." He continued, "As long as your truck is sitting in the road disabled, there are several individuals that are probably waiting in the truck stop parking lot looking for the right moment to come open the doors on the back of the truck to steal anything inside, or worse yet, rob you while they know you are stranded and can't get away." He pointed back at the restaurant and said, "Go back inside and don't come back out until your ride arrives." The driver moved the truck to "safety" and drove off into the night.

I felt a little more at ease knowing the only real risk was sitting across the road in the safety of the lights and cameras of a local business. We were safe inside, and the kids were being amazingly patient. Dad should have been arriving at any moment, and we could rest easy knowing that we should be in a safer neighborhood soon.

As I finished off the cold french fries the kids had not eaten, I was thinking about this gentleman who had just moved the truck from the road and disappeared without any compensation at all. Was it a good Samaritan or a guardian angel that had helped us? I'm not sure, but I was sharing with the kids the compassion he had demonstrated by helping to make sure we were at least a little safer. The kids were tired and beginning to drift off to sleep as we watched the workers sweeping and mopping the floors.

The moment of quiet reflection ended abruptly when a worker walked over to our table and told us they were closing. I asked how much longer they had until all of their work was complete and shared that my dad should be pulling in at any moment. I pointed across the street to our broken down truck and looked at the employee who, by this time, had a look of helplessness in his eyes. He said, "The manager says that you have to leave." I walked swiftly to the counter and asked to speak to the manager and began to plead my case to her. She only shook her head and said, "Company policy says we can't have anyone other than employees in the restaurant after we have closed." I pointed over at my two babies who had fallen asleep in their seats and said, "Please, my dad will be here before you guys get finished cleaning." Thinking she would have a little compassion I continued, "Look, you know this is not a safe area to be stranded with small children, so please let us stay inside until he gets here." She crossed her arms and said, "I don't make the rules but I have to follow them to keep my job." I gathered the kids, and we walked out of the restaurant and stopped just outside the door as the manager turned the lock.

Thinking the light would give us a little security and protection, we stood there with all senses heightened peering into the shadows wondering what would happen next. The manager had turned and walked away and within minutes the glow of the inside disappeared. We had now been joined with the rest of the darkness. I was trying to calm myself with prayer but I was also fighting back my desire to beat on the door and let the manager know exactly how I felt. The only thing stopping me was the idea that it would only draw more attention to us.

Fortunately the wait only lasted about 10 minutes because my dad came off the interstate like he was leading a pack of racecars. He stopped in the middle of the road and began to look around somewhat confused. When we spoke last, I had told him we were sitting safely inside, and now that he had arrived, he noticed it was completely dark in the restaurant. He spotted the truck and slowly pulled over to where it was now parked. I grabbed the hands of Brianna and Dawson, and we made our way back to the broken down truck.

Dad had anticipated the problem with the truck and had already made his way to two different auto parts stores that stayed open late. He informed me that they didn't have the right part but he was going to try and make something work. We locked the kids inside the truck, popped the hood, and dad went to work like he was on the pit crew of a NASCAR race team. I stood watching shadows pass between the trucks and, at times, move in our direction. Dad slammed the hood and instructed me to get in the truck, start it up, and head back to the store. I'm still thinking, "The part dad installed isn't an exact fit but don't worry, dad has a way of making things work with what he calls, 'southern engineering.'"

Dad's last words as I climbed into the truck were, "I hope it makes it." I looked over at the kids and they were piled on top of each other and sound asleep. I pulled out of the parking lot with great relief and began our trek back to the store empty handed. The Christmas trees somehow didn't seem important anymore. We made our 45-minute journey back to the small town where our store was located and both Dawson and Brianna woke up because of the smell that was entering the cabin. The wrong sized belt dad had installed had begun to burn due to the rubbing against other parts of the engine. I cut across a parking lot across the street from the store and, just as I topped the crest, the truck died again. We coasted the rest of the way into our own parking lot toward the back of the store and finally came to a stop. I turned the key, shut off the lights and just sat there in the darkness. I turned to look at the kids, and they were both rubbing their tired eyes when Dawson said, "Well that was fun!"

Fun isn't quite the word I would use to describe this adventure. However, I would definitely tag the word "eventful" on it. There were so many lessons learned from that night that have been the topic of conversation for many years. Things happen when you least expect them. Angels, or good samaritans, are alive and well on the earth and sometimes these heavenly beings can appear in the form of a tow-truck driver. Unfortunately, compassion and common sense are often overshadowed by a person's desire to follow the rules. This legalistic mentality can cause a person to miss an opportunity to provide a safe haven for one of God's children. Finally, the most important lesson Dawson, Brianna, and I learned that night was this: "When things appear to be dark and dangerous, there is power in prayer; God is still in control."

We finally made it to the Farmer's Market to get more trees, but this time we made the trip in the safety of the daylight. God is light, and light is good!

Thanksgiving Trepidation

Thanksgiving is a time of just that, giving thanks. One particular Thanksgiving had something included that I hope is never invited to ours, or anyone else's special day.   Trepidation! When trepidation shows up you become fearful because of an undesirable outcome. The roots of the word trepidation can be traced back to a meaning of fear and trembling. Fear? On a Thanksgiving Day that is normally full of family, fun, food, and football? Impossible! Only family and friends come together on such a joyous occasion, right?

The Thanksgiving meal was set on the table with much anticipation in the air. Each of the children talked about their favorite item on the table that year. Some loved the dressing, others the Heavenly Hash, while others talked about how much they really don't even like turkey at all. The winner every year is probably the deviled eggs. Everyone loves the deviled eggs. This year was no different than any other because by the time we all sat down for the meal, several eggs had disappeared. Looking around, there were some really quiet children sitting perfectly still, but looking perfectly guilty. They would smile with yellow deviled egg filling in their teeth and still deny any involvement in the missing eggs.

This year we had been experiencing an unusually warm autumn, and Thanksgiving Day had brought us some of the prettiest weather of the season. Dawson was a young boy who was full of energy with a need to stretch out after sitting for a long period of time. As we were sitting at the table, we exchanged places with the turkey. At the onset of the meal, the turkey was stuffed. By the end of the meal, we were the stuffed ones. After the conversations, laughter, and food, Dawson asked to be excused from the table. I reminded him that he needed to remain seated at the table until everyone else finished eating. He reminded me just how beautiful the weather was outside. I knew the sun would be setting soon, so I allowed him to leave the table and go enjoy doing what boys do best: run, jump, and get dirty. He bounded out of his chair with gusto and ran out the door to play as much as possible before darkness set in.

We had a busy day ahead of us, and I decided that Dawson should come inside, take a bath, and go to bed so that he would be rested for the long day that awaited us tomorrow. I walked to the door and hollered his name, "Dawson!" Nothing! Only the birds answered from the nearby trees. I called out again, drawing out the syllables, as any good dad would while calling for a child. "Daaaaaaw-sonnnnn!" Still nothing. I stepped out further onto the porch and whistled for him. The children knew the sound of my whistle, and it was well known, if I whistled, then they should come running while announcing their movement toward the door. A simple, "Coming!" was more than sufficient. What I heard now was a deafening silence. Even the birds had quit chirping as if to listen for an answer. I walked to the side of the house and began calling his name again, and it was then that our friend "Trepidation" arrived. A parent's heart has the ability to drop to his stomach and climb into his throat at the same time. I hurried inside to Dawson's bedroom to find a well made but empty bed. I began recruiting others to help in the search for Dawson, but we weren't making any progress. Worst-case scenarios began filling my mind, and fear continued to rise. I returned to the front yard and began walking down the road calling his name over and over. Still there was no answer. Nearly thirty minutes had passed and not one of us could find Dawson. Had we been so careless to allow him to go outside to play alone and then did we not hear his distress? Had he asked to go to a friend's house that lived down the street, and we had one of those parental moments of answering a question without really paying attention to the question? Whatever had happened, Trepidation stood close by to put its two-cents in. There are moments when you begin trying to remind yourself what shirt and pants your child was wearing on this particular day. His shirt was blue, no... red, no I think it was blue with white stripes. Fear was hovering as I turned and ran back to the house wondering what the next move would be. Do I call the neighbors? Do I get in the car and comb the neighborhood? Worse yet, do I inform the police at this point?

Entering the house, I was determined to search every square foot before I sounded all the alarms. I returned to Dawson's room and looked in the closet, under the bed, in the toy bin, everywhere! My search moved into the next room, and the next, and the next, until I had examined each room thoroughly. I even pulled back the shower curtains to see if maybe he was playing his own version of hide and seek. The only room that I hadn't looked in was the master bedroom. I knew the clock was ticking if he really were missing, so I moved quickly. I opened the door to the captain's drawers located at the end of the bed. This was a hiding spot we had utilized many times while playing indoor hide-n-seek. Nothing! I walked past the bed into the master bath only to come up empty-handed. As I walked back through the master bedroom, I passed the bed that had been neatly made that morning with all of its pillows stacked in a well-organized pattern. That's when I saw it! A foot! Not an entire foot, but just the end of the foot sticking out from under the pillows on the side of the bed. The soil-stained dingy sock was a stark contrast to the decorative pillows, pristine pillow shams, and bright duvet. I walked over and grabbed hold of the tiny foot and quickly pulled a slumbering little boy out of his peaceful sleep.

Startled, Dawson looked up in wonder with a look of, "Why are you here? Why would you wake me up so abruptly?" I snatched his little body up from the bed and began to hug him while fighting back tears. I repeatedly exclaimed my love for him while he still had this questionable look on his face. The fear was escaping my body, and peace was returning to take its place. However, part of me wanted to interrogate him, but why? It really didn't matter why he had decided that beneath a mound of pillows, this would be the best place to find sleep. I remember times in my own childhood that hiding places unintentionally became sleeping places. I know now how my mother felt when she would search for me in those moments.

Trepidation had invited itself to the festivities this year without permission. We hadn't set a place at the table for it, asked it to bring a dish, or entertained the idea of it showing up in the most unforeseen circumstance. Fear had decided that it wanted to fellowship with our faith and then tested our patience relentlessly on that day. In the future, sleeping under the pillow mountain was considered off limits and forbidden. The only fear that could exist on Thanksgiving Day from the day forward is this: Fear of not being able to button your pants from eating too much, or fear on the part of the turkey who laid his neck on the chopping block so willingly. Okay, maybe not willingly, but I am thankful that Trepidation moved on and giving thanks had taken its place.

"Peppermintality"

Often times in life we do things that are not wise,
intelligent, or even in our best interests. We get so
involved with the idea of instant gratification that we
don't realize that our actions could be as harmful as
losing our life over it.

Easton was a small boy who had the idea that
peppermint candy was worth dying for, literally!
Every Sunday morning we would show up early to
church in our typical chaotic fashion. There were six
young children at the time and each of them had their
own agenda when we walked through the doors of the
church. Some would take off running to find their
friends, others would head in to listen to the music,
and yet some would stay right by my side the entire

time. Easton would stay close to me until he had his escape fully planned, and then he would stealthily slip away. Easton wasn't allowed to run around and find his friends. Not without adult supervision! Easton suffered from "peppermintality" syndrome. Now, I know this isn't a real disease or sickness, but he was obsessed with the idea of consuming peppermints in mass quantities. We had asked every usher we could find to not give Easton any candy because he had a tendency to choke on it. Easton always tried to stay one step ahead though. Nothing was going to keep him from getting a piece of peppermint candy if he thought he could do it without detection. I began to question if he wasn't somehow addicted to peppermint.

The ushers would pass out peppermints as a small gesture of welcoming the people as they arrived to church. The people who served as ushers and greeters would change weekly, and Easton learned how to work this to his advantage. He knew which ones we had discussed our concerns with, and he would target the poor unsuspecting ushers whom we had not. Easton would get his peppermint candy and quickly run to a secluded place, unwrap the candy, and toss it into his mouth to enjoy all of the pleasures a peppermint could possibly bring. Too many times his ecstasy would be short lived. Somehow, he would swallow the candy, and it would get lodged in his throat, causing him to begin choking. For a child who wasn't very verbal, this game of charades had high stakes and consequences. When the candy would get stuck, Easton would frantically search for anyone to help him! At times, the Heimlich maneuver was necessary to dislodge the peppermint. This happened far too many times for comfort, and each time Easton would promise to kick his candy addiction. This "peppermintality" was serious! He knew what could happen, yet he constantly went back for more. He was willing to roll the dice as to whether he would get choked or not. Enough close calls finally got the attention of the head usher, and the decision was made to ban the passing out of candy to small children. Of course, a little wisdom could have been applied sooner, but who knew a kid could be addicted to peppermints to the point that he would continually return and knowingly ask for more after he had had so many close calls?

That inevitable moment in church life had arrived, and it was a sad day for many of the congregation who depended on the mints for their own comforting moments. Others wondered how they could continue on without mints to mask their pungent coffee breath. The day the candy would disappear from the pockets of the ushers and greeters was jokingly referred to as, "The Easton Rule." I'm sure parishioners both young and old grieved this day along with the local dentist. For us, the parents of a child that suffered from "peppermintality," it was a beautiful day.

A Box Full of Cool

"Daddy can I please, please Daddy, can I?

Those are the words I heard when my daughter
Ashton was about 10 years old. She had decided that
she "needed" some new shoes and this "need" could
only be filled with something called Birkenstocks. I
had never heard of this brand but soon found out, "All
the cool people wear Birkenstocks!" Well, at least
according to my daughter with her 10-year-old
perspective. Obviously, I would never wear those or
know about them because I wasn't young enough and
definitely not cool enough to join the fad. These
shoes were priced just over a hundred dollars at the
time, and I knew I had never spent that kind of money
on shoes for myself, let alone a child that was
growing by leaps and bounds and outgrowing clothes

and shoes almost daily. "But Dad…" Those two words became prominent in her vocabulary because I was obviously out of touch. Every time I would try to reason with her about the cost of shoes during this time in her life I would hear those words, "But Dad!"

Time passed on, and I thought I had dodged the Birkenstock bullet, well at least for a moment. She came to me one day and exclaimed, "Dad, if I take my birthday money and put it with some money I got for Christmas, I will have enough to buy my Birkenstocks!" "But are you sure you want to spend all of your money on shoes?" I asked. I spent time explaining that shoes, clothes, cars, and general "stuff" weren't what made somebody "cool." It fell on deaf ears because she only believed HER Birkenstocks awaited her, much like Cinderella's carriage. I gave in and said yes to the shoes knowing this was going to be a lesson learned either by her or by myself and that it would come with a price tag for one, if not both of us.

Nearly $120 later, my daughter became one of the coolest kids on the block. I never knew a pair of shoes would garner that much power and attention. The "cool" factor had definitely been stepped up! I think she began to walk cooler, talk cooler, run cooler, study cooler, do homework cooler! Okay, okay maybe three out of five isn't so bad. The last two were a bit of a stretch. Education cool wasn't the goal for this pair of shoes to accomplish. The shoes had changed her entire world, or at least the perception of it.

My little entrepreneur visionary child had learned a lesson with this box of cool.

Birkenstock blues. There was a dark side to wearing these life-changing shoes. They kept getting dirty. What? Shoes getting dirty? How could this be? She began coming home upset because her shoes had a water spot, dirt, or, heaven forbid, filthy soles. I tried to explain to her that this happens to all shoes. "But not shoes I paid over a hundred dollars for Daddy!" I knew that if I had paid the hundred-dollar price tag for these same shoes, this dedication to their preservation would have never happened. Well, at least not to this level of protection. How do I know? I saw this same lesson when I was a younger man. I watched my sister have the car keys taken from her until she repaid my dad for a set of tires she had burned up. My dad had witnessed my sister "burning rubber" racing another car through town. He knew a lesson had to be taught, but more importantly learned. We often don't take care of things we have no investment in. My daughter did have an investment in these shoes. As a matter of fact, she had her entire life savings invested. She wanted these shoes to stay store window ready forever.

The shoes had brought stress into her life, and she had finally resorted to keeping them in their original box. "Cool" obviously doesn't stay on the shoes if they aren't on your feet. Apparently these cool shoes also had the power to steal someone's joy and peace while making life miserable. We all know these shoes really never had the ability to bring joy, happiness, or even coolness. But as a young girl that was attempting to "fit-in," they had supernatural powers and abilities.

These shoes had somehow gone from being the talk of all of her friends to residing in a box in a dark corner of a bedroom closet. I have to give her credit though; she eventually realized that she had friends who needed that touch of "cool" in their lives as well. She saw an opportunity to at least recoup some of her hard-earned money and sold her prepackaged box of cool to a friend. I asked her if she thought that was a good idea. She did not understand my point of view and quickly reminded me how much money she had spent on those shoes. I told her, "Your uncool friend might not realize the stress these shoes could bring her." She informed me by saying, "Dad, shoes, clothes, and cars won't make you cool, but my friend could now be cool too at a much lower price!" My little entrepreneur visionary child had learned a lesson with this box of cool. The lesson she wasn't expecting to learn was this: having a little hard-earned cash in your pocket can give you a little something extra in your step, and your "cool" doesn't come in a box or from a store.

Leading Beyond Bedtime

My daughter Brianna was our second child and what many would label as our "strong-willed child." If I asked her to move left, she would move right. When asked to sit down, she would stand up. Don't even attempt to silence her because she would get louder and louder just to make sure that it was her will that was accomplished and not yours. I could request she sit down until I was blue in the face, only to have her finally sit and look up at me with that look of, "I'm still standing on the inside."

Bedtime had its own challenges. Regardless of how early or late Brianna would go to bed, she still had a few more hours of energy to burn off. She would lay in bed and just recap her day to herself. Well, I say to herself, but I really mean "out-loud" to herself. She would finish discussions from earlier in the day, answer questions, win arguments, complain about siblings, plan for the next day, talk about anything and everything except sleep. Most importantly though, she would sing!

She would lay in bed and start off singing a few children's songs she knew, then onto making up her own songs, but finally she would get to the songs I loved the most, worship songs. Brianna had an incredible knack at a very young age of memorizing songs. Of course nursery songs and stories were pretty easy to learn with repetition. Learning the French tune, "Ah, vous dirai-je, maman" Mozart later used in his "Twelve Variations on "Ah, vous-dirai-je, maman," made learning "Twinkle Twinkle Little Star," "Baa Baa Black Sheep," and the "Alphabet Song," really easy. But that's not what I'm talking about. Brianna would sing entire songs from beginning to end, every chorus, every bridge, and every measure as if she had written them herself. Not quietly in the darkness of her bedroom, but loud as if she were performing before hundreds! Without a microphone! She owned the stage located at the top of her bunk beds much to the annoyance of her younger sister who just wanted her to stop singing so she could go to sleep.

Leading the congregation is what she had mastered. Although her sister was the only one in attendance and very disgruntled with her leader, I knew there was an even greater Audience present in this sanctuary called her bedroom. God and a multitude of angels surely showed up for every worship service she led. The entire house would already be slipping into a slumber while she invited the One she knew would faithfully come into her personal worship and song service. "He'll show up," she once said. "He always does." He's like that you know. He created us to worship Him, and He inhabits our praise. As a matter of fact, we were designed to fulfill His eternal plan, to love our neighbor and to love Him. I learned many years ago that worship gets God's attention. Obviously, Brianna had tapped into this as well.

Brianna would invite the congregation into the service by asking them to repeat after her, "This is the day that the Lord has made. I will rejoice and be glad in Him." Then she would break out into song as if they had all followed her instructions and had joined her in this ministry moment.

How do you discourage that kind of behavior in a child? Why would you? I would remind her that she needed to sleep and that she would need to finish her singing so that her little sister could get some sleep as well. She would always tell me, "I've got just one more song Daddy!" So one more song it was. Brianna is grown and married now. I don't know if she has only one more song every night. Nor do I know if her husband has to ask her to stop singing so he can sleep. But I do know that I cherish those moments during her childhood that she taught me to follow her into worship with a childlike faith. She would fall asleep in the arms of her heavenly Father leading the congregation well beyond bedtime. And I would soak in the afterglow from another room knowing she was planting seeds for the future and probably doing more spiritual battle from her bed than many do on their knees.

Let's "FACE" the Facts

My dad often said to me, "Lessons learned the best are often those that cost us the most." I've found that statement to be very true throughout my life. All too often, the mistakes I have made in life had very little bearing on my life unless there was a large price tag attached to them. Those are the lessons that hurt! The lessons that knock you back on your heels and cause you to wonder why you can't learn just a little quicker in life.

Growing up offers many lessons to be learned, especially from those moments hanging out with all of the neighborhood friends. Good kids, bad kids, kids from all backgrounds and circumstances. You want your child to learn about diversity and difference, but even that sometimes comes at a price.

I think every neighborhood has "that kid" that has a tendency to either have some of the worst luck ever, or just seems to carry trouble around in his back pocket. Well our neighborhood had several of those, but one stands out to this day. One that taught us a very important lesson about making wise choices and remembering that your parents often make rules you don't agree with or understand, but they are there for your protection.

Every time this kid would come around our house, somebody would get hurt! I tried to not place the blame on him, but it wasn't just sometimes, but EVERY time! I had gotten to the point of turning onto our street, seeing his scurrying silhouette departing our yard, and quickly wondering what was broken, who was injured, or what had been stolen. I hated feeling this way about a child because I wanted to give him the benefit of the doubt. However, facts are facts.

I gathered my children around and gave them the

history of each event that had taken place when our neighborhood "friend" was in or near our house and pointed out how much turmoil surrounded him when he came to visit. Of course, my children only looked at me with their heads slightly tilted to the side as if I were speaking a foreign language. I knew that one of his shenanigans would surely have a high price tag attached if I didn't demand that he not be allowed to come to our house anymore. My words fell on deaf ears, and my very own children didn't see the harm of this friend's presence. Goodness, he was like a stray dog that had been given a few table scraps and now desired more food being tossed his way because the kids had fallen in love with him. I finally set my foot down, demanded that he never return, and warned the children that he was NEVER allowed to come on our property again! Never! Never, ever! I couldn't afford one of my own children getting injured by his escapades.

It didn't take long before our "friend" returned. Actually, it was the very next day that I received a frantic phone call from one of the kids telling me Brianna had gotten injured. I was only a few miles from home and arrived within minutes. As I turned into the driveway, I spotted Brianna on the porch with her hands over her face, sobbing uncontrollably. I raced to her side and as she lowered her hands my heart dropped. She was bleeding from her hairline to her chin. Not having received all of the information at this point I asked what had happened. Brianna began telling me about her running down the street and tripping over her own feet before stumbling to the ground. I immediately began trying to determine how to handle this emergency. I had never seen anyone with a "road rash" covering his or her entire face. She had gravel, grit, dirt, and sand covering her open wounds and I knew we needed to head to the emergency room immediately. However, I felt like there was something I should be doing to help my little girl. But what or how? I began removing the larger gravel from her face and quickly realized this was much worse than I could even imagine.

I loaded Brianna into the car and headed to the emergency room. Fear began to fill my mind that she would have facial scars that could devastate a young girl. With all of the injuries I had personally experienced throughout my own life and all of the "boo-boos" I had seen with my children, I knew that a scab would often leave lasting impressions and scars that last a lifetime. But a scar or deformity on a young girl's face? I couldn't imagine what the long-term effects were going to be.

So, like any good father, I sped to the emergency room but felt the need to gather the facts along the way. Brianna held to her story about losing her balance and tripping over her own feet, but in a large family that includes a lot of younger children, the facts pour out like a waterfall of information. One of the siblings gladly gave up the culprit! Yes! Our neighborhood "friend" had returned. Yes, "that kid!" But to hold true to their understanding of my now set in stone rule, he didn't actually come in the yard, but stayed in the street in front of the house. Well everyone knows that if he stayed in the street, well then, he really hadn't come to the house. There seems to always be a loophole available for those unwritten rules. I turned to Brianna and said, "You didn't trip over your own feet and fall did you?" She hung her head and said, "No sir." I pressed into the interrogation knowing there was a common denominator that tied our "friend" into the equation. Apparently, he offered to give her a "piggyback" ride and when she jumped onto his back, he lost his balance, stumbled forward, and Brianna's face absorbed the asphalt along with the fall. Looking into the mirror of the sun visor, she came to the realization that disobedience often leads to dire consequences. She began to cry even more when the fears I had experienced earlier had now been transferred to her by the image she had seen in the mirror.

We spent the entire evening in the emergency room as the nurses attempted to clean the wounds and remove the debris from Brianna's face. It was a tedious process, and they medicated her in order to keep her from experiencing too much discomfort. The prognosis didn't sound good. The nurses and doctors suggested there could be some extensive permanent damage and scarring. There was nothing more we could do but pray.

Two days later we prepared to head to our Sunday morning church service when Brianna pleaded not to go because of her injuries. I reminded her that although we have things we don't want to explain to others, life continues. Though often embarrassing, we sometimes learn, not only from our mistakes, but also from our admission of poor decisions. We arrived at church and were immediately greeted by many who, while cringing, asked about the details of this almost grotesque appearance. Many gawked but one stood apart. The woman I would lovingly refer to as "Grandma." This was an elderly lady who had graciously offered to become my grandmother after my own had passed away. She was not only a woman who had love for everyone, but she was a prayer warrior. A woman who knew how to garner the attention of heaven, Grandma hugged Brianna tightly and began praying for her healing and that all scarring would completely vanish. But then she stopped and said, "Lord, leave a small reminder for Brianna so she will remember the importance of obedience, for obedience is better than sacrifice."

One week later to the day, we walked into church with Brianna's face completely healed. Scanning the congregation, I had to find Grandma to show her what had miraculously happened in this short period of time. Needless to say, Brianna had no problem walking into church this day. She was excited to show off what had amazingly happened. Brianna had been so excited to see the progression of her healing each day that she had missed one important detail. Grandma rejoiced with us and praised God outwardly for the answer to her prayer. I told her I knew God would hear her prayers, sit up, take notice, and then answer them. She held Brianna's face in her hand and reminded her to remember God's faithfulness every time she looked into the mirror. Brianna agreed and said that she would. Grandma told Brianna that God had left a small reminder of his goodness. I remembered Grandma's prayer for Brianna and how she had paused and asked for a small reminder to remain. To this day, Brianna has a small scar that, unless you are aware of it, goes unnoticed to everyone except her. It is still a small reminder of the benefit of walking in obedience to the Father. Not her earthly father, for that was a lesson that came with time and more learning moments. However, she now understands that for every decision or action, there is a consequence or reward. It took her "facing" the facts in order to learn this valuable lesson, but it is one that cost her something and will stick with her until the end.

3 B's: Brothers, Battles, and Bonds

Senior year has finally arrived for my oldest son and he is ecstatic about his last year of varsity football. Several players are returning, enthusiasm is in the air, and this is a large junior and senior class that have been battle tested and ready to finally have a winning season. It had been several years since the Lions dominated and posed a threat on Friday nights. But this was Dawson's year! His senior year! The year he would lead the battle and preserve the "Lion's Den!"

Exodus!

Exodus is defined as the mass departure of people. A

flight or evacuation of many as a means of escape or migration. An exodus is the only word I can find to describe what happened at the beginning of this school year. Nearly a dozen athletes departed from the sidelines of this football team that had one of the best chances of "going all the way" this upcoming season. The grass was apparently greener in other pastures and it appeared the grass would be slowly dying and not utilized at all for those left behind. The football team had been crippled before they could take their first snap. Driven by many disgruntled parents who never quite understood classifications of schools in athletics, the call for mutiny had begun. The school had been placed in a higher classification because of the number of students who were attending when the realignment had taken place. The enrollment count was just over the maximum students allowed to remain in the lower classification. Therefore, this was one of the smallest schools represented in this region. The majority of the starting lineup would partake in this mass exodus. The program was officially doomed to become just a faded memory. Friday night-lights would not shine for these young men entering their senior year.

In comes a seasoned coach that had seen a tremendous amount of success during his many years in and around the state. Stepping out of retirement to take on the impossible task of resurrecting this phoenix of a football program, he met with the remaining players, students, and parents. He shared his vision and desire to keep the program alive, knowing just what it would take in order to breath life back into football for these young men. My sons were included in his mission. He had to convince the seniors and upperclassmen that they didn't need those that left prematurely. He had to bring leaders and true athletes onboard in order for others to actually buy in also. Dawson was very influential among his peers and was one of a handful of seniors that remained. Easton, a freshman, was one of the most talented athletes in the school, and Zephan, although only a 7th grader, was built with just enough grit to step onto the field with nearly grown men and take on varsity teams around the region. Dawson was the first one to buy in because he desired to protect "his house!" He hadn't spent his time training in the Alabama heat and humidity of summer to merely give up what his team had worked hard for during the last several years. The Hopkins' brothers were going to defend the "Den" together. A trio of brothers that didn't realize the changes it would bring to their lives.

The team was eventually built with a hodgepodge of 7th to 12th graders. Athletes, students, kids scared half-to-death, and those who dressed out but prayed they would never be called on to go into the game. For the boys on the sidelines, this was a mission fueled by determination to protect their honor and that of the school. For the parents in the stands, it was a time of constant prayer that their son wouldn't go to the hospital amidst this chaos. The team went 0-10 that year. The average loss was by 48 points and seven of the ten games were lost with one or less touchdowns being scored by the Lions, five of those being complete shutouts. It was painful to watch as a football fan, but even more painful as a parent sitting in the stands watching his sons playing both offense and defense and never showing a desire to retreat until they were carried off the field. This was truly a class of young boys who grew to become men this year under the lights of Friday night. Young men that understood fighting for honor of their alma mater to be that of determination, dignity, and sacrifice.

My sons came together like warriors on a battlefield. Easton had been thrown into the position of quarterback and running back with limited previous experience in either of those positions. Zephan also stepped into the running back spot along with special teams. The one thing they both had in common was their big brother Dawson. He was a force to be reckoned with on the field. Dawson knew he wasn't the most naturally talented football player, but what he lacked in talent was made up with a work ethic that would put many college or pro players to shame. Dawson had earned the nickname "Dawg" because he was like a bulldog that once engaged, his battle didn't end until he had his opponent flat on his back. Watching boys twice his size line up across the line from Dawson was fun to watch. They would approach the line for the first time, point at Dawson, laugh with their teammates, and then find themselves looking toward the heavens. They would rise to their feet with a lot of "smack talk" vowing that it wouldn't happen again only to find themselves lying on their backside just moments later. Only this time, Dawson would be on top of them face-mask to face-mask promising them he would win the battle every time. Dawson overwhelmingly kept his promise to these giants and made sure they knew he would return with a vengeance until the final horn sounded. Easton became the playmaker that year. He somehow would find yardage in traffic when it seemed impossible. I felt as if Easton had become a magician, for he would somehow disappear into the crowd and then miraculously appear out of nowhere to gain another ten or twenty yards. He would do this all night but somehow the Lions could never capitalize on the gains. Easton has natural ability that can only be a gift from God. He can walk onto any playing surface of any sport, have a ball tossed into the mix and be instantly successful. Many lessons of the game were obvious to Easton. The most important one was that his big brother Dawson made things happen in front of him. Easton felt a sense of security with Dawson blocking for him. If someone got to Easton on one play, Dawson would make him pay on the next. One important lesson Easton did learn that year was that success on the field creates responsibility off the field. Suddenly, Easton had become a rock star among the little kids at his school. They had bestowed him with the crown of coolness. Fortunately, Easton accepted the wisdom I gave him about this newfound fame. I taught him about many athletes that go on to become superstars and decide they don't want to be role models. But it is out of their control! Those that begin looking up to you do so because they want to be like you, have the success you have, or they desire to experience the popularity you are experiencing. Easton was humble enough to know that he needed to make sure he kept that in check. Zephan, being the youngest of the boys, saw less playing time than his big brothers, but when he stepped on the field he played like he was a fifth year starter. He moved down the field on special teams looking for that freight train called the punt returner to come charging at him. If they were going to make it to the end zone on a kick, they would have to come through him. These Friday night brother-warriors consumed the public address system with each passing play. The name "Hopkins" was included in every announcement during the game.   A "Hopkins" caught the ball, gained the yards, or helped make the stop on every down.

Watching your sons get beat up on the football field can be extremely painful to watch. We made several trips to the emergency room along with many other parents that year. I don't know of a single young man on that team that could've been dragged from his commitment. This group of boys, now growing into young men, had been transformed into warriors that knew the battle might be lost, but losing the war was unacceptable. These boys had come together to be trained as soldiers. They learned how to battle the enemy and stepped out of the locker room every Friday night knowing they were considered to be the underdog. That meant absolutely nothing to them. They marched onto the field as if they were on their way to a state championship season. This group of boys had taken on the task to perform when the deck was stacked against them. But this isn't a game for boys, but of men! And men they had become.

My sons weathered this storm and survived! If you ask any of them today if they have regrets of stepping up to the challenge knowing they would take a beating every game, their answer would be a resounding, "No!" This season created a bond between them they had never experienced. You know, brothers often love to pick on one another and fight. This experience bonded them together like they never expected. Teams are made of people who join together to accomplish a common goal. But for the Hopkins' boys, this was a time to come together as players, teammates, and most importantly brothers. To watch my sons meet in the middle of the field after the last game of the season, embrace each other and weep, taught me one of the greatest lessons of life. Battle-worn brothers are in the war far deeper than a physical commitment. These warriors had body, soul, and spirit completely invested to fight for one another. This fight may have been in a game that happens on Friday nights, but its implications run much deeper because this game teaches lessons about life. These were the "3 B's of Brothers, Battles, and Bonds," but we now have a fourth "B" added, "Boldness!" They now know that they can come against adversity in life and fight through it with a boldness that was learned on the field that almost didn't see the lights on Friday nights. These men can look back as they face adversity in life and know that battles create stronger warriors. Warriors that are bonded for life to have a greater vision and win wars!

D=Dedicated, Determined, or Driven

You can describe my son Dawson with any one or a combination of these words: Dedicated, Determined, and/or Driven. He has always been one who works hard and is determined to complete a task. I could always point him in any direction and tell him to go and he wouldn't stop until he couldn't go any more.

As a young boy, Dawson would spend the entire day working with me. That was one of the perks of being self-employed. He is my oldest son and after having three girls, a boy was a breath of fresh air. We could wrestle and do "boy" things. Kicking rocks, playing with sticks, picking up bugs, and poking dead things like mice and frogs was the norm when we were together. He was my little running buddy and never got much further away from me than the length of my shadow.

The exception was at our produce store I operated with my parents. Dawson would go outside by himself to the back of the store and dig in the dirt, stack blocks, and play ball. We spent a lot of time out there enjoying some father-son activities, but often Dawson would venture off and entertain himself with various activities. Unfortunately, the business was very seasonal and during our peak time of the year he had to create a lot of his own entertainment while we worked diligently inside. He was all boy and never lacked for imagination or ingenuity. He would often come running in the store to announce his new discovery or creation out back. I would slide out there to see what was going on, give him an "attaboy" or two, and hurry back inside before I was missed.

One sunny spring day, Dawson came inside and was overly excited about something outside. He grabbed my hand and told me to hurry outside so he could show me something. I informed him that I was busy and couldn't come out there at that moment but would make it happen just as soon as I got a chance. He continually tugged on my hand and insisted that I would be excited if I just came out there. Once again, I told him it would have to wait. He looked at me with sadness in his eyes and turned to walk outside. You know, there are just times that business has to come first. I had responsibilities to fulfill, and my attention to the customer was paramount at the time. Or at least I felt that it was during that moment. I finally finished what I was working on and walked outside to see him sitting on the back steps. I asked him what he needed to show me, and his enthusiasm was gone. He told me it didn't matter anymore. I tried to explain myself to him, but he wasn't buying it. It took quite some time to convince him that I really did want to see what he was so excited about, and life began to dance again in his eyes. We walked behind a storage building behind the store to where an old abandoned road ran through the property. He

turned and said, "Are you ready daddy?" I wasn't
sure what I was supposed to be ready for, but I said,
"Of course I am!" He ran around the corner of the
building and reappeared riding an old broken down
bicycle I had found in the dumpster and had left
behind the store. I had hoped to, maybe someday, put
some training wheels on for him to learn to ride. I
guess I had waited too long.

I stood in awe watching him attempt to make the
bicycle go in a straight line. He was riding a bike!
No training wheels! No help! Nothing but sheer
determination to learn. I began to cheer for him as he
swerved down this abandoned road, and I ran along
behind him in case he needed me. But he didn't need
me! Unfortunately he hadn't needed my help
learning to ride a bicycle. He had learned how to ride
by himself. That's when it hit me and in the midst of
my excitement, sadness overcame me along with this
stark reality; I began to cry. This little boy, without
the help of his daddy, had taught himself how to ride
a bike. I was proud of him, but I was crushed that, in

my busyness, I had missed the opportunity to be there to instruct, encourage, and celebrate his first success.

I purposed in my heart from that day forward to take the time to listen to my children. Although I had missed the opportunity to help my son learn how to ride his bike, I knew he would've probably accomplished that without me anyway. That's just the way he is designed and continues to forge his own course even to this day. The words dedicated, determined, and driven can all be summed up in one word, Dawson!

In the Deep

Several years ago we joined friends for a summer cookout and a much-needed time of refreshment in their swimming pool. This was a typical hot and humid day in Alabama. Because of the size of our family, we rarely received an invite to any social gatherings. Families with a couple of children are safe to invite to parties because their presence does not overwhelm the population. When your family bypasses the third child, you enter the "peculiar" category. At this particular time, we had four children and were officially labeled "one-of-those" families. Who has that many children on purpose in this day and time? When our family showed up we basically doubled the size of any party. Still, we gladly accepted the invitation. I was thankful for any opportunity for the kids to be outside of the house.

Being a parent with multiple children, you develop great counting skills because you have to take inventory constantly. Admittedly, with more adults around, those constant "head-check" habits get a little lax. This was one of those days! Adult conversation had been absent from my social life for quite some time, and I was soaking up some intellectual engagement that was long overdue. Suddenly, I felt the need to locate all of the children. In a crowd of nearly twenty kids running like caged animals who tasted freedom for the first time, trying to find my own children became almost impossible. I would count, one, two, three, wait… Let's try this again. One, two, three…Hold on! One, two, three…. Did I count that one twice? No, just once but wait, where did the other one go? Okay, okay I've got this. Maybe the child that is missing is inside going to the restroom. No need to panic. Take a deep breath and relax.

The swimming pool setting is one of fun, excitement,

chaos, and pure happiness all at the same time. That is, until you can't find one of your children. Then it becomes an evil beast that is attempting to steal one's joy, peace, and sanity. My mind raced as I looked across the faces of all the children splashing around. Cierra, the baby girl of the family, was still missing. A strange object caught my attention at the bottom of the pool. My mind immediately went to a deep, dark place when I realized it was my baby girl. My fears had suddenly become my reality. My baby was on the bottom of the pool, but she wasn't attempting to swim or move. How was she that deep and staying eerily still? With one hand stretching toward the surface as if she were reaching to touch heaven, I could see her face as clear as if she were sitting in my lap, safe in my arms while telling me about a special moment in her day. Since the day Cierra was born, people have complimented her for having beautiful, piercingly dark eyes. On this day, those same piercing eyes penetrated the depths of the water and made contact with mine. I jumped feet first into the water and grabbed her outstretched arm. I pushed off the bottom of the pool, rocketing us both to the surface. As we broke the surface, she inhaled the biggest gasp of air possible for a little girl her size. I frantically swam with her to the edge of the pool. I quickly assessed the situation and was ready to put to test the CPR training I had received so many times but had never expected to use. As I held Cierra in my arms, I asked one of those rhetorical "parent" questions that are extremely ridiculous. I asked, "What in the world were you doing standing on the bottom of the pool?" She looked me in the eyes and said, "I was talking to that man, daddy!" I said, "Man? What man?" Cierra looked back at the bottom of the pool where she had been standing and said, "The man who told me that I was going to be okay."

I don't know who the man was in the pool telling her that everything would be okay. It could've been a guardian angel or it could've been Jesus. I do know that she wasn't afraid, and she knew that whatever happened, she would be okay. If God hasn't given us a spirit of fear, and she was at total peace, then I believe the voice in the deep end of the pool that day was definitely heavenly in nature.

There are days you may feel like you are drowning. You feel like you are in the deep end of a pool completely engulfed by the world. Although you may know how to swim, you feel paralyzed by feelings of inadequacy, worthlessness, or fear. You may have lost all hope of salvation or rescue, but God has not forgotten about you. He sees where you are, and He wants to calmly reassure you that everything will be okay. He wants to whisper in your ear that He loves you and has a plan for you. When all around you may seem dark and hopeless, He is the constant reminder that you have tremendous value. Reach for Him. Listen for Him. Trust Him. He will never abandon you. Take a deep breath…and rest!

Disobedient Dive

"Lessons are often learned the hard way!" That's exactly what my father said to me when I was a young boy. I guess it is just human nature to try and push the boundaries in life and see exactly how much we can get away with. For children, those boundaries are a reminder that brings comfort. Children need to be aware of these boundaries so that they can understand safety. When they choose obedience and conform to the rules, they experience protection. When they choose to break through the boundary lines, they lose that level of protection and enter into dangerous territory. I've always said that you can stand on the balcony of the twentieth story of a building with no reservations. The railing sets a boundary line and, therefore, provides protection and comfort. If I were to remove the railing from the balcony, the twentieth story becomes more intimidating. Not only is the feeling of security gone, but peace and joy have probably left as well. We need to know where the boundaries are in life. A child on that balcony would probably run up to the railing, look over the side in amazement, and then begin climbing the railing. This gesture would terrify any adult because of the dangers associated with climbing the railing.

Naturally, adults understand the risks of pushing boundaries.

When my children were younger we lived in a house that had an in-ground swimming pool. Along with a swimming pool come many boundaries and a well-established set of rules to keep everyone safe. Of course you have the standard rules in place like: "No running around the pool," "No flipping off of the sides of the pool," "No glass items in or around the pool," "No diving into the shallow end," and of course, "No peeing in the pool!" A rule we added was that there shouldn't be any bikes in or around the pool area. Of course, the reason for this is pretty obvious, but for some it was just another boundary to challenge.

One summer, I had gone out of town for the week, and the weather was perfect for swimming. Everyone had gathered around the pool when my son Zephan decided that a bicycle would be the perfect addition to swimming pool fun! Zephan was probably seven years old at the time, and a bike is just part of a young boy's identity. It was a symbol of freedom to him with the wind whipping through his hair as he glided along effortlessly. Add a little water to the mix and you have the ultimate formula for "coolness."

Zephan cruised around the pool a few times before others began telling him that he wasn't supposed to have his bicycle in the pool area. He didn't care! As long as his "cool" was gaining momentum he was content with his disregard of the rules. Cruising along, his siblings began informing him that they were going to tell on him. "I'm going to tell Dad," became the mantra of all those around the pool, and

Zephan would continually reply, "I don't care!"

In the day of technology there is always the ability to gather evidence when someone is breaking the rules. Today was no different. The camera came out and the recording began with the same mantra as before. "I'm telling Dad if you don't get off the bike and get it away from the pool." This only empowered Zephan and he sped around even faster. As they informed him that they were recording, Zephan replied again, "I don't care!" He smiled as he went by and then decided to loop by one last time and wave at the camera. On the video you hear, "I'm recording this and I'm going to tell Dad you are riding your bike around the pool." Zephan waved at the camera with a huge grin on his face. But then his "cool" ran off the track! He lost control of his bike, his foot slipped off the pedal, and he careened directly into the swimming pool. All caught on video! It was definitely one of those moments that should have been sent directly to the television show "America's Funniest Home Videos."

Needless to say, Zephan was mad and stormed inside while everyone else laughed uncontrollably and attempted to regain their composure. But isn't that how we all are? We push against the rules because we want to spread our own wings. We even blatantly rebel against what we know is right. Many times we want to yell out, "I DON'T CARE!" but in our attempt to maintain our maturity we try to not look too crazy. We should all be thankful that our blatant disobedience isn't recorded for the world to see. Like Zephan, when "cool" falls off the track or even into a swimming pool, we often get mad and run away. Disobedience often creates division and isolation. It creates a wedge. We know how to properly behave, but in reality, we want to exercise our freedom of choice.

Two lessons were learned that day. First, Zephan learned that breaking a rule that is in place to protect you can lead to instant repercussions and, secondly, video can haunt you for years. We all laugh about the incident now, but it was a lesson Zephan learned that boundaries were really in place to keep him and others safe.

Hide and Go Crazy

Playing and being silly with the children is one of the
most important things you can do before they grow
up or before it becomes "uncool." Playing games of
tag, kick the can, board games, charades, cards,
make-believe, or even just riding bikes can be a blast.
However, one game that stands out the most to me is
the game of hide-and-seek. To make it even better,
playing hide-and-seek inside on a rainy day is the
best. Creativity comes into play and when one person
is found, everyone becomes the seeker.

Trying to hide inside the house is challenging because
with children that span a multitude of years, the little
ones always want to hide with Dad. You know, Dad
always has the best hiding places. It's difficult to
keep the little ones quiet when they get the "giggles."

Little do they know that Dad always has a few hiding places that he saves for those really intense games. Many of those spots are utilized only briefly until the game drags on, then the strategic move to a known location occurs so you don't give up the secret hiding spot.

The hide-and-seek game to determine the "world champion" of all hide-and-seek players was about to go down. We had an all-star group of competitors on this rainy day and the indoor championship was about to begin. Ashton, Brianna, Cierra, and Dawson were all ready to dethrone the all-time champ, Daddy!

The entire house was available to the competitors. Nothing was off limits! Some of the simplest places were the best. Many rounds were won by simply hiding in the shower or behind a door. However, my hiding places were being discovered and no longer useful in the game. The older kids were on to my tricks and I began losing too many rounds to still declare my dominance. I had to resort to the hiding places of all hiding places.

It was the final round, and I slid into the master bedroom where often the game was not allowed, but this night we had opened all boundaries. The bed was sitting atop captains' drawers and had a tunnel that went end to end under the bed. The tunnel was concealed with a door and we stored very few items underneath. It was a tight fit for a grown man to slide into this tiny space, but I had to make it work. The king could not lose his crown to a bunch of kids. I slid in backwards into the dark and pulled the door closed behind me. I tried to scoot backwards quietly as to not alert my pursuers. I could hear all of the other competitors being picked off one by one. The problem now was that all exposed players were now looking exclusively for me.

I could hear the pitter patter of Cierra, the youngest girl's feet as she came into my bedroom and began walking around the room slowly opening everything from closet doors to drawers. I guess spatial reasoning isn't well developed for a small child. In her mind, I could surely fit into a drawer. Suddenly the door of the captain drawers opened and all I could see were the big brown eyes of Cierra staring into the darkness. I hoped I could be quiet long enough that she wouldn't recognize me in the shadows. A scream of excitement sounded and suddenly everyone arrived at the end of the bed. Cierra was the first to yell, "Let's all get in here with Dad!" I came alive and yelled, "Okay, you found me! Game over!" Let's all get out!" Little did they know, Dad has an extreme case of claustrophobia! In case you aren't familiar with claustrophobia, it is the extreme or irrational fear of confined places. My irrational fear is beyond extreme. I suddenly began hyperventilating as the tunnel grew from one occupant to five. I felt like I could've thrown the entire bed through the ceiling as my heart raced. I began to beg the children to exit but none of them moved. I grew quiet and tried to gather my thoughts and find peace once again in what seemed like an eternity. Silence fell upon all of us and then I heard a small voice say, "Isn't this fun

Daddy?" Cierra was having the time of her life while I was feeling like my life was running out of time. Slowly the kids exited one by one, but it didn't seem fast enough. I had already broken into a cold sweat and could feel my heart pounding against the floor as I slid toward the end of the bed.

That was the last day I ever used the captain's tunnel as my secret hiding place. As a matter of fact, I never entered there again. I couldn't take the chance of being trapped and suffering from my claustrophobic meltdown. Cierra found my favorite hiding spot that day, and I would gladly turn the spot and the crown over to Cierra to begin hiding in more obvious places. I thought I would go crazy in that moment but hide-and-seek played inside on a rainy day isn't worth losing your peace over. That's just crazy!

Let's Ask Dad

Fatherhood is one of the most difficult jobs I have ever had, but it is definitely the most rewarding one. For all of the single moms and dads out there, my hat goes off to you. I have been there, done that and have the t-shirt. Well actually there isn't a t-shirt but, as you well know, there are the lessons and scars that come along with the challenges of parenting alone. Giant Kudos to the "step" parents who step into what can seem like an impossible role at times. I've never been a fan of the term "stepparent" because I believe parenting is a full-time, fully committed, responsibility and shouldn't be referred to in a slightly removed position of less importance.

Let's Ask Dad began as a passion project of wanting to become a published author. It turned into a reflection of the life of my older children. The stories are too numerous to share, but I am confident that the life experiences will continue to multiply in number. I am blessed to have eight beautiful children. Ashton, Brianna, Cierra, Dawson, Easton, Zephan, Hudson, and Beckett. As the oldest children are all growing into wonderful adults now, I know they will surely provide lots of laughs and even more stories as grandchildren become part of the bigger picture.

My wife Anne came along after the breakup of my first marriage and amazingly stepped into a parenting role that I know I probably would've never considered. That may seem shallow, and it probably is, but Anne provided the nurturing and woman's touch that was void in a single-dad's home. I have often said that Anne was either crazy or a Godsend. Maybe she is a little of both! Who takes on the role of wife and mom to a man and six young children unless they are?

Anne and I now have two more boys, Hudson and

Beckett, that are nothing less than a miracle. These little guys have enriched our home and brought about a reset moment as we begin the whole process again. Many men my age are settling into to their role as grandpa, I am blessed to have grandchildren and my own children at the same time. Does it require a lot of energy? It does, but in my own humble opinion, there is no greater joy than being a father. I believe raising my own little boys will also help me focus on helping the grandbabies to become everything God has called them to be and not just take on the role of spoiling them. Oh, they'll get spoiled enough by Anne! I have no doubt about that happening.

I hope "Let's Ask Dad" has encouraged you, but more importantly, I hope you have seen a man that is merely trying to be the best dad he can be. There is nothing I can do without God being the main focus of my life. Through all of the moments, I have attempted to point my children toward Jesus. Even when I, their earthly father, have fallen flat of my face, I have tried to point them to the moment when I was at my lowest and sought the Father of all Fathers. I hope each one of them remembers that I don't have all of the answers, but I do know how to get back up. I have a plentiful amount of wit, wisdom, and positive encouragement, but our Abba (Daddy) father is the one who has all of the answers to all of the questions and isn't surprised when we ask him. So, throughout the good times and the bad, don't forget to "just ask Dad."

Special Thanks

I am indebted to my dad who is the most honest and hardworking man I have ever known. He has singlehandedly taught me more about life than any educational institution possibly could. He continually exudes character and integrity and is an official graduate of the "School of Hard Knocks."

A special "Thank You" to my children Ashton, Brianna, Cierra, Dawson, Easton, Zephan, Hudson, and Beckett who put up with their zany father who wants them to know and experience joy, peace, and happiness that can only come from living a life that includes loving God, loving people and serving others.

I also want to thank my wife Anne for supporting me in my endeavor to become a published author. If not for her continued prayers and support, this project would have never been possible. She has been the cheerleader that continually encourages me and countless others to chase after God and walk in the purpose He has for each one of us.

Finally, I want to thank my Lord and Savior Jesus Christ to whom I owe everything.